Meal Prep Guide

Quick & Healthy Meals for the Busy Family
(Includes 40 Meal Prep Recipes)

By

Pamela-Anne Kinney

Table of Contents

Introduction

I would first like to thank and congratulate you for choosing this book "Meal Prep: Guide to Quick & Healthy Meals for the Busy Family". You will find the information most helpful in your journey to becoming a pro in the preparation of healthy meals for your loved ones. You will be glad to hear that it is not difficult to master becoming good at meal prep. I have also included in this book some wonderful and easy to follow recipes to get you started on the road to totally mastering the art of meal prep!

Many people think that meal prepping or planning ahead is reserved for large families only. Well, I am here to tell you that this is just not the case. You can involve many different aspects of meal preparation into your routine These include time consuming tasks like planning and chopping up of your foods. There is also an assortment of other work such as blending up foods the night before that you will use the next day for breakfast.

Some people love using meal prep so that they have an easy-to-prepare meal when they get home from work. We will cover the different aspects to meal prepping in the book but first, let us begin with Chapter 1 which discusses the benefits to meal prepping.

~ Pamela-Anne Kinney ~

Chapter 1: Benefits of Meal Prepping

You might be thinking to yourself why should I bother to meal prep? You probably do not think that you can become that organized in the planning of your meals but with a little effort, you can. There are benefits that you may have not even thought about yet.

One of these is the potential saving of money. You will be able to make large cuts in your grocery bill by buying in bulk. Just because you buy in bulk will not mean that you must process all of it at once. You can do a week's worth of meals, then freeze the ingredients you did not use. You will certainly get better deals when you buy your meat in bulk. One of the great joys of meal prepping is you are going to have a variety of meal choices to choose from. Many larger families have already been practicing bulk shopping to help with the overall savings on the grocery bill. You too can now also adopt this habit to help with your meal prep.

Meal prepping works great for those that have people in their family that likes to eat different foods. You may have a child that is a very fussy eater. You can make special meal preps for your child so that you know they are going to eat their meals. You have the option to cook different things at your meals with very little hassle. This way everyone would be happy with the food they are eating and no food is going to waste or at least less food will be wasted. If people are eating meals they enjoy, there will likely be less food left on their plates at the end of the meal.

When you do meal prep you are in better control of making portions; you can pre-weigh your meals to make sure that you are getting the correct portions and are not overeating. In meal prepping, you will weigh the correct portions of your foods, you will then see it before you what the right amount of foods you should be eating. This is very handy especially if you are trying to lose weight or are on a special diet plan. Doing this is going to help teach you what the proper size portions are that you should be eating.

Using meal prep will come in very handy if you are on a diet. This can help you to avoid snacking on other foods such as junk foods. With meal prep, you will be taking control of what you are putting into your body in the way of food choices. This can help you to gain a more positive and healthier attitude towards food that can help you to lose that excess weight. It will also help you to avoid binge eating on those hard days that you might feel extra hungry.

Meal prep can help you to form regulated eating patterns where you have made meals that are healthy that will cover you for all of your meals so that you are not eating the wrong foods. This often happens to many of us that live a hectic and busy lifestyle—it is well worth the planning of meal prep to cover meals during these busy times. We will then be less likely to turn to junk food or fast food. If you skip meals, this can actually lead to weight gain as your hormones become imbalanced and your metabolism is lowered so it is important to make a point of eating meals regularly. When you have healthy meal prep foods on hand, you will be able to achieve this more easily.

Another great thing about meal prep is that you are able to customize it to your lifestyle; there is flexibility with meal prep. You can decide the type of meals that you want and how much time you are going to put in to prepare them and set that time aside when it suits you. Studies have also shown that people that have time to prepare meals will make healthier choices than those that feel so rushed that they skip meals altogether. Choosing to prepare healthy meals using meal prep will make you tend to choose the healthy foods over what is the quickest.

Meal prepping is a great way to help battle the temptation of turning to the fast and junk foods. You can feel good in knowing you are going to head home after a day of work to a nice home-cooked healthy meal rather than calling up the nearest take-out restaurant.

Chapter 2: How to Meal Prep in a Few Easy Steps

In this chapter, we will take a look at the best tips and advice for you to become competent at meal prepping in no time! Once you are on the road to becoming good at meal prepping, you will never look back. You will very likely continue moving forward onto the next great set of healthy meal prep recipes!

1. Buy in bulk
Where or whenever you can, always buy food supplies for meal preps in bulk. It is going to be a lot cheaper to do so and it will certainly make it easier for you to decide on meals for the evening. You can meal prep some of it, then freeze the rest to use for another meal prep session; perhaps the following week.

2. Prioritize your meals
Do this especially when you do not have time to prepare all of them at once. You need to pick the most important meals to complete first. If you are someone that likes to have snacks, make sure that you chop plenty of fruits and veggies to snack on. This is preferable to trying doing a big meal prep when you are short of time.

3. Set aside time to do meal prep

If you are cooking large batches, then you will need to put aside a day each week to get this done. Make sure that you are doing it when you do not feel rushed so that you can prepare the best meals possible.

4. Cook large batches of food that you are fond of

You do not want to make a large batch of food only to find that it is not something that suits your taste. Try new recipes in small amounts before you decide to cook them in batches. Cook foods that you are familiar with at first in batches then eventually expand to other new foods.

5. Slowly build up food variety

You do not have to cook 20 different food options in your first week. You can always start off with having one meal for dinner one day and have the leftovers for lunch the next day. It will take time to build up different options so approach it in a slow manner; don't feel rushed.

6. Bake veggies & meat on the same tray

You can save yourself fewer things to wash up by cooking your veggies and meat on one big tray in the oven. The juices will create a nice sauce that you can use on the meat to prevent it from going dry when you reheat it.

7. Make some smoothie-cubes

Add smoothie mixture to the ice-cube tray, allow them to freeze then add them all to a freezer bag. You can fill the ice-cube tray back up, repeat until you have filled your freezer bag with smoothie-cubes. Now you can take a couple of cubes out the night before and put them into a glass and some milk to water them down.

8. Multi-task

While you are cooking dinner, use the time that you are waiting for the food to finish cooking to chop up some veggies for your meals for the next few days. Once you get multi-tasking under your belt, you will find it much easier to get more things done within a shorter timeframe.

9. Spice up your meals

Keep your meals full of flavor and interesting by adding spices to them. You can make your meal taste so much better just by adding some spices or allowing your meat to soak in a marinade.

10. Keep prepping when you can

Just keep in mind that anything that you do in the preparation of a meal ahead of time is considered meal prep. This include chopping up veggies to cover you for the next few days.

Of course, you want to make sure that you are getting a well-balanced meal. So making your prep meals as healthy as possible is something that you should also consider when choosing them. Once you have decided what you are going to eat, you need to sit down and write out a shopping list. I find one of the easiest ways to write out a shopping list is to have my recipes right in front of me. This way you will know the exact quantity of ingredients you will need to purchase. If you have not had time to write out a shopping list, just keep in mind that you want to get fish, meat or protein with at least two of your meals per day.

Buying your meat in bulk is the best option as you can freeze it. When buying your fruits and veggies you should figure out the quantities needed for a three-day period. Even if you shop for a week, you can freeze any fruits that are reaching expiration to use in smoothies.

Buying herbs can get expensive, so the best way is just to buy them per recipe that they are needed. You may even choose to grow your own herb garden, so you have fresh organic herbs at hand when you need them.

You want to try stay away from foods that are too processed. It is best that you totally avoid junk foods like ready meals or chips. Try not to keep other foods in the house when you are in the process of getting into the habit of eating your meal prep food. There will be less temptation to eat other things when they are not readily available.

You may decide that you want to start using meal prep with one meal a day such as dinner. Then once you are more comfortable with the setup, you may decide to do all of your meals in this fashion. Learn to become adventurous with your eating habits by trying new foods; perhaps you might create a new dish using your leftovers.

Chapter 3: How to Eat Clean with Meal Prepping

One of the best ways to keeping yourself healthy is to use foods that are healthy in your meal preps. Many of us work outside of the family home and when we come home, the last thing we want to do is to start working on meal preparation in the kitchen. We want to be able to also offer our loved ones' healthy meals that will be easy to prepare. If you are trying to lose weight or are just wanting to have your diet includes better choices, using meal prep can help you to stick to the healthier choices in foods. If you prepare meals for your weekdays that are made up of healthy foods, you are less likely to put aside your dieting regime when the meals are basically ready and waiting for you to eat them.

You can take a few hours in a day each week for this. I myself do my meal prep on Sundays; I prepare all my meals for the following week. This works well for me as it provides me with healthy meals and snacks for the week ahead. This practice enables me to incorporate clean eating in all my meal prep as well as keeping me away more from fast foods and processed foods. You might think that it seems like a lot of work, but believe me, it is well worth spending those couple of hours getting clean, healthy meals prepared ahead of time. I know it is great to have meals that I can feed my family that are going to be full of good clean foods instead of feeding them too much fast foods and processed foods.

Often when I am doing clean eating meal preps, I will do two days' meals then will make a couple more on Wednesday for the rest of the week so that nothing goes bad. I find it much easier to stick to healthy clean foods when I have made the meals ahead of time.

You can do foods such as the following:
- Whole roasted chicken, shredded use in your salads, pasta dishes, sandwiches, etc.
- Boiled eggs—I will boil a dozen and use them for breakfast or snacks through the week.
- Peanut butter—add to apple slices or in your smoothies
- Tomato & Basil Soup
- Celery, cucumber, and carrot sticks
- Chopped up cauliflower and broccoli to use in stir fries
- Roasted vegetables for salads and pasta dishes
- Quinoa – add to salads
- Whole wheat pancakes – for breakfast
- Prep freezer bags of chopped mixed fruit to use in smoothies

You will find wonderful healthy meal prep recipes in Chapter Six.

Chapter 4: How to Create a Healthy Meal Plan

We all are looking for ways that we can feed our loved ones the weekly meals that are going to be healthy and keep us from getting bored with the act of cooking at home by saving us time in the meal prep. The suggestions and tips in this chapter will help you learn how to create a healthy weekly meal plan that should not only save time, money but more importantly lead to enhancing the habit of doing meal prep on an ongoing basis.

What is meal planning? This is when you organize yourself to cook a meal, whether it is breakfast, lunch or dinner. This is the plan you make before you do your shopping for groceries. How long of a period that you want to cover in your meal planning is of course entirely up to you. Many people will plan their meals for a month at a time. Personally, I prefer to make a weekly meal planner. What you must do is set a goal that is attainable, enjoyable and effective for you. There are also people that love to look through cookbooks, or look at recipes online or clip recipe ideas from magazines.

An important part of the whole process is to anticipate the meal planning procedures and the ultimate goal. Meals are not just about eating to survive, but they are also a chance to create new culinary experiences for yourself. Just cutting a sandwich into a new shape is bringing out your creative side. When a meal looks visually appealing, there is a higher chance that people will eat and complete that meal. Find ways that you can become inspired to the point where you are looking forward to cooking a meal. When you become animated about cooking, you will be excited about meal planning.

You must find what works best for you; there is no right or wrong way to doing a meal plan. You need to find a way that is effective and easily fix into your schedule. Don't waste too much time trying to discover the perfect system; the system is just a tool to serve you. The primary focus should be the meal itself that you are planning. A great way we love to socialize is eating some good food with friends and loved ones. Enjoying each other's company while we nourish ourselves.

Get Inspired

1. Spend some time each week looking for new recipes.
Why not check out some online websites where you can find potentially great recipes to enjoy with your loved ones. Grab some cookbooks and leave some sticky notes on the special recipes – get inspired!

2. Find an easy way for you to keep recipes stored
Find a way to save the recipes that work best for you. Perhaps you could keep a folder of recipe collections on your computer or you may prefer to hand write them in a book you keep in your kitchen. Make it an easy and simple system to maintain.

3. Ask your family members what they would like to eat
Find out from your loved ones the kinds of meals that they would really enjoy having. You will gain great pleasure in knowing you are making a meal they truly look forward to.

4. Check the weather forecast

The weather forecast can help you to decide what food you are going to be interested in eating. For example, if it is a cool and damp day you might feel like having some nice hot soup that day.

5. Keep a meal journal

A great way that I personally get inspired is from things that I have cooked in the past. Look back and see the types of dishes that you use to cook and the ones that you are cooking today. I make my weekly meal plan on the weekend. My grocery list is based only on the ingredients needed for the meals in my weekly meal planner.

Getting Yourself Organized

6. Begin with a calendar

Now that you find yourself getting inspired on what to eat and what you would like to cook for the coming weeks or at least the next few days, you can choose to make it very simple and basic, or you may want to make it more elaborate. That of course will be left entirely up to you. The more important thing is to write or record those things down and perhaps have a meal planner or calendar.

As for me, I often take time to look through cookbooks to find new and exciting recipes to try. I also find them online and then print them out and add them to my meal planner. Continuing adding to my personal preferred list of meals means that my planning calendar can be quickly filled up.

7. Theme nights are fun

I always tell my loved ones that each day's meal is either Indian, Italian, Chinese, Asian, Greek, etc. I based this on whatever the main dish is going to be. For example, if I am preparing spaghetti that night for dinner, I will refer to that evening as 'Italian Night." This makes the daily preparing of the meal a little bit more fun. Sometimes I will say its Vegetarian Night if I am serving a meal with no meat or Soup Night, if soup is going to be the main course.

8. Make a shopping list and choose a day for shopping
Many people that are successful with meal prep make use of shopping lists when they go to the supermarket and try to stick to the list. This gives them certain targeted foods that they are going to get and helps to keep them from buying other foods they do not need. Learning to stay tuned into what foods you need that are on your shopping list is key to being successful in meal prep and planning.

9. Check to see what is on sale
I will often gear my weekly shopping list around what types of foods are on sale that particular week. A good idea to keep in mind is knowing what fruits and vegetables are in season.

10. Eating Leftovers
I am someone that likes to cook in bulk and then sub-divide that big cook into a few meals to do throughout the week. I will often use leftovers for lunch the next day as well.

11. As soon as you get back from the store, begin to prep food
Start to wash veggies, chop and roast them. Brown newly bought sausages for pizza. Shred some zucchini for some yummy quick fries or slice up sweet potato for sweet potato fries. Stack up your storage containers in the fridge and then admire this great organizing of the meals that you have just accomplished.

I try to do most of my meal preps as soon as I come home from the grocery store or supermarket. This include taking out my block of cheese and shredding it right away. Once completed, they are put into a freezer bag. We now have shredded cheese for the week ready to use for times such as Taco Night.

12. When it comes to freezing, be strategic
The freezer is a great ally that can help make your meal planning so much easier. I like to make a big pot of spaghetti sauce. I will use half for this week's Italian Night and I will freeze the other half for a meal in the near future.

13. Don't overstuff the fridge

When you shop weekly just for the ingredients you need to cover your weekly meals, you will find that your fridge will not be so full and overflowing with things. You want to be able to see what is in the freezer that needs to be cooked soon. If the fridge is too stuffed, you will not be able to easily see what is in it.

14. Cook components of your meals

You can cook selected components of meals such as doing a pot of tomato sauce that will later be used in three different meals. Or cook a whole chicken that you can have for dinner that night and then use the leftovers for lunch the next day. The main idea here is to cook in larger portions even if this is just for part of a meal.

15. Keep your pantry well-stocked

It is much easier to prepare meals when you are well-stocked in things such as olive oil to cook your meals in and the right spices you need or tomato sauce. Always try to have fresh herbs at hand and at least a lemon.

Chapter 5: Keep Meal Prep Simple & Low Cost

In this chapter, we will look into how to keep your meal prep cost low so that you can come up with healthy meals while cutting down on expenses at the same time. One great way using meal prep will save you money is that it will cut back on the amount of time you are going to eat out at restaurants and fast food places just because you are too tired to go through creating a whole meal when you arrive home from a long day at work.

By taking some planning into your week, you can make your meals at home with ease and speed and still provide your loved ones with a good healthy meal. Most of all, you are also going to save a ton of money when you stop eating out as much. With just basic planning, your entire meal prepping will actually be low cost in addition to being simple. These will be discussed a bit later in this chapter.

Keeping some staples or key ingredients around is going to be key in making your life a bit easier. Then you only have to go shop for the ingredients you need for your meals that you have included on your weekly shopping list.

To Be Stocked at All Times

Here are some items you should keep stocked in your fridge at all times.

White or Yellow Onion
This is one of the most used ingredients I depend on in my meals preparation. Onion is not expensive but it can add so much flavor to most of your meals. It is something that is definitely worthwhile making sure you always have in your kitchen.

Fresh Garlic
One of the easiest things to add to dishes is a couple of cloves of garlic. This is also another effective and inexpensive way to make your food taste great. You can use garlic in all kinds of dishes such as stir fries, soups, and salads.

Olive Oil
This is a good item to stock up on especially when it is on sale. Watch out for when it is on offer at a good price, then stock up. Using olive oil is a healthier alternative to using margarine for cooking your meals. You can, of course, also use it to make an excellent salad dressing such as balsamic dressing.

Whole Wheat Pasta
Wheat pasta is yet another staple that is good to keep in stock. It will store well for ages so buy it in bulk when it is on sale.

Eggs
Don't be tempted to buy brown eggs that cost more because you think they are more nutritional than white eggs. In truth, they both have about the same nutritional value. So it is advisable to stick to the cheaper costing white eggs and save yourself some money without losing any nutritional value doing so.

Chicken or Vegetable Stock/Low Sodium
This can come in very useful when you are cooking quinoa, rice or couscous dishes. They do not take up much storing space and are inexpensive.

Cans of Tomato Sauce
Look for the tomato sauce that is on sale, then buy a bunch of cans to stock up on. I find this a particularly useful item in quite a few dishes.

Bananas
These are a great source of potassium and are fairly cheap. They are a good fruit to keep on hand for daily fruit source. However, you might not want to buy too many each time as they do not stay fresh for too long.

Rice or Couscous
I often wait for the rice to be on sale, then I buy a big bag to stock up. A large bag can normally last for months and it will fill you up for pennies.

Salt and Pepper
These are basic as a staple to add some flavor to your meals. I myself use sea salt and buy peppercorns and use a pepper grinder.

The items I mentioned above are all basic stuffs that you can build your meal prep ideas around. They are not going to cost you a fortune even when buying in bigger quantities.

Suggestions for Meal Prep Breakfast

Yogurt Parfait
You can make a yummy inexpensive healthy breakfast just by mixing some yogurt, fruits, and some granola.

Breakfast Smoothie
This is a great way to use ripe (including even over ripen) fruits or spinach that is wilting. I usually make myself a batch of these that will last for up to three days. Get creative with your ingredients; the combinations are endless.

Everything Omelets
Another highly recommended way to use leftover veggies from the dinner of the night before. Add some salsa to give it more zing.

Crepes
These can be so yummy and just as easy to make as pancakes though they are a lot thinner. The recipe is in Chapter Six under Snack Recipes.

Suggestions for Meal Prep Lunch

Red Onion Pizza Sub
This is a quick and easy way to make yourself a pizza sub. On a half slice of French bread, halved it lengthwise. Just add pasta sauce on top and your favorite pizza ingredients. Then leave it in an oven or microwave oven for the cheese to melt. Recipe suggestion is provided under Lunch Recipes in Chapter Six.

Broccoli & Peanut Sautee
This is easiest one of the quickest lunch you can prepare. Just a fast pan fry and you have a ready-to-eat healthy lunch. The recipe in the Lunch Recipe section in Chapter Six.

Cheese and Ham Quesadilla
Here is another quick and healthy lunch. The recipe can be found in the Lunch Recipe section in Chapter Six.

Eggwich
You can't go wrong with eggwich, a sandwich that is quick and very easy to prepare. The recipe in the Lunch Recipes section in Chapter Six.

Chickpeas & Chorizo
This is also a great healthy and quick lunch. The recipe can be found in the Lunch Recipe section in Chapter Six.

Suggestions for Meal Prep Dinner

Winter Beef Stew
With a cheap cut of meat and some inexpensive veggies, you can make an extremely tasty and low-priced stew. Recipe is in the Dinner Recipes section in Chapter Six.

Veggie Fajitas
One of my all-time favorite dinner meals is Veggie Fajitas. It is a healthy meal that most people will enjoy. The recipe is listed in the Dinner Recipes section in Chapter Six.

Simple Pita Pizza
This is another low-cost item which is both healthy and easy to prepare and tastes yummy! Recipe in Dinner Recipes section in Chapter Six.

Szechuan Chicken Stir Fry
This is one of my own personal favorite meals that is inexpensive, quick and easy to get ready. Go to Chapter Six for the recipe.

Mango & Grainy Mustard Salmon

Here is a relatively cheap and yet easy to prepare meal for dinner. Done right, it can be extremely tasty and nutritious. The recipe is provided in the Dinner Recipes section in Chapter Six.

South American Whole Wheat Burrito

This is a meal that your loved ones will request every now and then. It is very inexpensive and easy to prepare. The recipe is in the Dinner Recipes section in Chapter Six.

Suggestions for Meal Prep Snack

Chickpeas
Chickpeas are very inexpensive and healthy. You can quickly make a great snack with these. I love to snack on roasted chickpeas with vinegar and sea salt. You will find the easy-to-follow recipe in the Snack Recipes section of Chapter Six.

Nutella and Peanut Butter Sandwich
This is a tasty quick snack when you are on the go. It can help a lot in holding you until meal time. All you need is the bread of your choice, peanut butter and Nutella and you are good to go.

Instant pickles
Cut up a few slices of cucumbers and add vinegar and a few slices of bell pepper. Quick healthy and an inexpensive snack.

Tortilla Dipping Chips
Take a tortilla and cut it into triangles; one per person. Top with olive oil, salt, pepper, and your choice of shredded cheese and bake until the cheese has melted.

Chapter 6: Meal Prep Recipes

In this chapter, you have a wonderful collection of prep meal recipes covering breakfast, lunch, dinner and snacks. If you want to make enough for two meals, just double the recipe ingredients for the single serving meals. The serving numbers of the recipes vary; just make the necessary adjustments according to your needs. You might want to make a big batch so you can freeze some for another day or just do a single serving for a quick and easy meal.

Breakfast Recipes

1. Crepe

Servings: 1

Ingredients:
- three-quarter cup of whole wheat flour
- two eggs
- one tablespoon of butter, melted or a light oil
- pinch of salt

- one and one-quarter cup of milk
- add a topping such as blackberries and a touch of sugar-free maple syrup

Directions:

It is best to make the crepe batter the night before so it is ready for use in the morning. Begin to mix the flour, milk, salt, eggs and butter in a large mixing bowl until there are no lumps. Cover the bowl and put it in the fridge.

When you are ready to cook your crepes, put a large pan (as large as you want your crepes to be) over medium high heat with a teaspoon of butter or oil in it. Once the butter has melted and the pan is hot, use a ladle or a cup so you can add the same amount of batter to the pan each time you make a crepe. You want to put only enough batter to coat the bottom of your pan. Once the edges of your crepe begin to brown, remove from the pan and place on a holding plate. Fill the crepes with your preferred topping, roll them up and enjoy.

Suggestions:

One of my personal favorite toppings is using Nutella and strawberries. You can also make extra crepes so that you can freeze them for another day. These will make quick and easy freezer snacks anytime you need one.

2. **Everything Omelets**

Servings: 1

Ingredients:
- three large eggs
- one-quarter cup of old cheddar cheese
- one teaspoon of butter
- a handful of mushrooms, chopped
- one-quarter of a white onion, finely chopped
- one teaspoon of chives, freshly chopped
- salt and pepper to taste
- two tablespoons of milk
- salsa to taste

Directions:

Over high heat, melt butter in large pan. Once the pan is hot, add in the mushrooms, onion, chives, and a dash of salt. Cook until browned. In a large bowl, beat three eggs with two tablespoons of milk adding salt and pepper to taste. When the veggies have browned, turn down the heat to medium and add in the egg mixture over the veggies. Once the eggs have set, add in the cheese. Slide the omelet onto a serving plate and enjoy this yummy breakfast. Add salsa to taste.

Suggestions:

You can get creative with the types of veggies to add to the omelet. I often will use veggies that I have left over from dinner the night before. If you are trying to reduce your cholesterol, you can also use two whole eggs and two egg whites instead.

3. **Protein Pancakes**

Servings: 10

Ingredients:
- one cup of quick oats
- one cup of egg whites
- one cup of cottage cheese
- one teaspoon of Stevia, powdered
- one banana
- two scoops of pea plant based protein powder
- two teaspoons of cinnamon
- two teaspoons of vanilla extract

Directions:

Blend all the ingredients until smooth. Preheat a large skillet over medium heat. Grease with cooking spray. Pour the batter into the skillet and cook for five minutes on both sides.

Serve hot with nuts, fruits, cottage cheese or Greek yogurt. You can freeze pancakes in an airtight container for up to three months.

4. Buckwheat Waffles

Servings: 5

Ingredients:
- four tablespoons of coconut oil
- one-quarter of a teaspoon of salt
- one-quarter of a teaspoon of cinnamon
- one cup of buckwheat flour
- one large egg
- one tablespoon of coconut sugar
- one and one-quarter of a teaspoon of baking powder
- one teaspoon of baking soda
- one and one-quarter cups of buttermilk, shaken

Topping Suggestions:
- almond butter
- banana slices
- maple syrup, sugar-free

Directions:

Preheat the waffle iron. In a mixing bowl whisk buckwheat flour, baking powder, baking soda, cinnamon, sugar, and salt. In another bowl whisk egg, buttermilk, and melted butter. Pour the wet mixture into the dry mix. Blend until smooth. Pour the batter into the preheated waffle iron.

After its cooked, serve immediately. You can also allow some portions to cool so you can freeze them in a freezer bag for another day.

5. Baked Banana and Oatmeal Cups

Servings: 12

Ingredients:
- three-quarter of a cup of bananas, mashed
- two tablespoons of coconut oil
- one teaspoon of vanilla extract
- half a cup of soy milk
- half a cup of protein powder, vanilla
- half a teaspoon of baking powder
- half a teaspoon of baking soda
- one-quarter cup of applesauce, unsweetened
- one and one-quarter of a cup of rolled oats

Directions:

Preheat the oven to 350° Fahrenheit. Grease non-stick muffin tin with cooking spray. In a mixing bowl whisk banana, milk, applesauce, vanilla extract, and coconut oil. Add in the protein powder. Mix until well blended. Bake for 15 minutes. Broil for three minutes.

Allow some to cool so you can put them in an airtight container and freeze them for another day.

6. Muffin Sandwiches

Servings: 6

Ingredients:
- six slices of cheddar cheese
- six large eggs
- six English muffins split
- twelve slices of ham
- salt and pepper to taste

Directions:

Preheat the oven to 375° and lightly grease ten-ounce ramekins with non-stick cooking spray on a baking sheet. Crack an egg in each ramekin. Beat lightly. Season with salt and pepper to taste. Place in the oven for 12 minutes or until the egg whites are cooked. Place one egg into each muffin bottom half. Top with two slices of ham and one slice of cheese. Cover each with a top muffin half, creating a sandwich.

You can wrap them with sandwich plastic wrap tightly and freeze some for another day.

7. Spinach, Feta, and Bacon Frittata

Servings: 6

Ingredients:
- 6 eggs
- six slices of bacon
- half a cup of milk
- half a teaspoon of garlic powder
- half a teaspoon of salt
- pepper to taste
- half a cup of feta cheese, crumbled
- half a cup of onion diced
- one and a half cups of spinach
- one and a half cups of Yukon gold potatoes, peeled, diced
- one-eighth of a teaspoon of paprika

Directions:

Cook the bacon in a pan over medium-low heat until it is crispy. Remove from pan and place on a paper towel. Grease the pan, add the onion and sauté for a few minutes. Add in the spinach and sauté for three minutes or until spinach is wilted. Add to a bowl.

In the remaining bacon grease add in the potatoes, add some olive oil if needed. Fry potatoes until soft. Adjust the heat level to low. In the bowl with spinach, add in the milk, garlic powder, eggs, paprika, salt, and pepper and then whisk. Crumble the bacon into the bowl and mix. Pour over the potatoes. Cook without stirring until the eggs are almost set. Sprinkle in the feta cheese over the top, transfer to the oven and broil for three minutes until the eggs are set.

Cut into six pieces when it has cooled. Put each piece in its own freezer bag and freeze for future breakfasts.

8. Quinoa, Broccoli & Egg Muffins

Servings: 12

Ingredients:
- three large eggs
- two green onion sprigs, chopped
- one and a half cups of egg white
- one cup of quinoa, cooked
- one tablespoon of onion or garlic powder
- half a cup of Italian parsley, chopped
- half a teaspoon of salt
- half a teaspoon of pepper
- one-quarter cup of Mozzarella cheese, shredded
- one-eighth of a teaspoon of red pepper flakes
- two cups of coarsely chopped broccoli

Directions:

Preheat the oven to 350° Fahrenheit. Take a twelve-inch muffin tin and spray it with non-stick cooking spray. In a large bowl, whisk the egg whites and eggs for 25 seconds or so. Add in the mozzarella, cottage cheese, red pepper flakes, onion, garlic powder, salt, and pepper. Stir and add the broccoli, parsley, quinoa, and green onions. Mix. Fill the muffin tins three-quarter of the way full. Bake for 20 minutes. Broil for a few moments to brown crust.

Allow to cool and put into an airtight storage container and store in your freezer for up to three months.

9. Spinach, Sweet Potato & Egg Taco Bake

Servings: 9

Ingredients:
- six large eggs
- three small sweet potatoes, grate
- two handfuls of baby spinach
- one tablespoon of jalapeño seeded and minced
- black ground pepper and salt to taste
- half a cup of white cheddar cheese, shredded
- half a cup of almond milk
- half a teaspoon of taco seasoning
- one teaspoon of garlic, minced
- one-quarter of a cup of cilantro, fresh chopped

Directions:

Preheat the oven to 350° Fahrenheit. Line an 8×8 baking dish with parchment paper. Spray with cooking spray. Set aside. In a mixing bowl whisk eggs, salt, pepper, taco seasoning. Add in the milk, cheese, jalapeño peppers, cilantro, and garlic. Whisk and add in the spinach and the potatoes. Mix. Transfer to the baking dish and bake for about an hour.

Remove from oven and allow cooling. Cut and serve hot or cold. Put some in an airtight container to save for another day. It will keep in freezer for up to four months.

10. Banana, Berry, Oats & Quinoa Bake

Servings: 9

Ingredients:
- three ripe bananas, sliced
- two large eggs
- two cups of almond milk
- half a teaspoon of cinnamon
- one and a half cups of blueberries
- one teaspoon of vanilla extract
- half a cup of quinoa, uncooked
- half a cup of raspberries
- half a cup of steel cut oats
- two tablespoons of maple syrup
- dash of salt

Topping:
- non-fat Greek yogurt
- one-quarter cup of unsweetened coconut flakes, toasted
- one scoop of protein powder

Directions:

Rinse the oats and the quinoa about three times under running water until water is clear. Drain well. Set aside. Wash and drain the berries. Slice the bananas. Set aside.

On low-medium heat, stir the coconut until golden brown or bake in oven at 375° Fahrenheit until golden brown and set aside. In a medium bowl whisk the milk, protein powder, eggs, maple syrup, vanilla, cinnamon, and salt. Set aside.

Preheat oven to 375° Fahrenheit. Spray 8x8 inch baking pan with cooking spray. In an even layer layout blueberries, raspberries, and bananas at the bottom of the baking dish. Spread the oats and quinoa on top of fruit. Top with remaining banana slices. Slowly pour the egg mixture into dish. Sprinkle the top with toasted coconut. Bake for one hour.

Remove from oven and allow cooling. Cut into slices. Serve warm or cold. Top with a dollop of Greek yogurt. You can keep it in the fridge for up to five days.

Lunch Recipes

11. Red Onion Pizza Sub

Servings: 1

Ingredients:
- a handful of pepperoni
- six-inch slice of French bread, halved lengthwise
- a few slices of red onion, thinly sliced
- old cheddar cheese, grated
- three tablespoons of pasta sauce

Directions:

To save some money, use sauces that are on sale or those with less known brands. If they taste a little blah just add in some diced onion, bell peppers, and minced garlic. Add the sauce to the top of the bread slice and then top with pepperoni, cheese, and onion. Place on baking sheet and bake in oven at 375° Fahrenheit for ten minutes or until the cheese begins to bubble.

Suggestions:

You can always switch the pepperoni for something else such as eggplant if you want to make a veggie pizza instead. I make a few of these at a time so I can have a nice cold pizza for breakfast the next day. You might like to try using barbecue sauce to spice things up a bit.

12. Broccoli & Peanut Sautee

Servings: 1

Ingredients:
- two cups of broccoli cut into small pieces
- a handful of peanuts, unsalted
- a handful of mushrooms, thinly sliced
- few tablespoons of Szechuan Sauce or to taste
- one tablespoon of olive oil

Directions:

Heat the oil in large pan over medium-high heat. Add in mushrooms and cook for five minutes until brown. Add in the peanuts and broccoli and cook for another three minutes. Add in the Szechuan sauce and mix well and cook for an additional five minutes.

Suggestions:

The mushrooms in this dish are optional, but I find they add a nice meaty flavor to the dish. You could also use red or white onion and cashews instead of peanuts. If you have leftovers of chicken, beef or pork, throw these in.

13. Cheese & Ham Quesadilla

Servings: 1

Ingredients:
- two tortillas, soft shells
- four slices of black forest ham
- one-quarter cup of old cheddar shredded cheese
- one tablespoon of grainy mustard
- a few slices of red onion, thinly sliced
- enough olive oil to coat pan bottom

Directions:

Spread the mustard on one side of the tortilla shell and add the cheese, red onion, ham and cover with another tortilla shell. Heat olive oil in a pan over medium heat and then place the quesadilla in pan for about four minutes per side or until the cheese has melted.

Suggestions:

You might want to try salsa and sour cream instead of grainy mustard as your condiment. Another yummy option is ham and Swiss cheese with thinly sliced mushrooms. The red onion is totally optional.

14. **Eggwich**

Servings: 1

Ingredients:
- two slices of bread or pita bread
- two eggs
- enough old cheddar cheese or other cheese of choice to cover piece of bread
- one teaspoon of butter

Directions:

Heat the oven to 300° Fahrenheit to melt cheese on top of slices of bread. Have a pan over medium-high heat to melt butter and fry the eggs. Once the eggs have cooked, add the cheese. Place the eggs between the bread slices and enjoy.

Suggestions:

If you have some leftover lunch meat such as ham, turkey or roast beef, place this meat under the cheese on bread slices before you put into the over. You can even use buns for this recipe instead of bread. The choice is yours.

15. **Chickpeas & Chorizo**

Servings: 1

Ingredients:
- 125 grams of Chorizo, cut into coins
- ten cherry tomatoes, cut in half
- one 540ml can of chickpeas, drained and rinsed

Directions:

Heat a large pan over medium heat and add in the Chorizo. Fry up in five minutes. Add in tomatoes, chickpeas, a dash of pepper and cook for a minute or two and serve hot.

Suggestions:

If you have some leftover spaghetti sauce, toss it in with the tomatoes and chickpeas. You can also add other veggies of your choice to this dish such as mushrooms, green onion, bell peppers, and fresh herbs. You can make a nice lunch treat with this chickpea-chorizo mix by adding it to a piece of pita bread or other bread of your choice.

16. Chicken Bake

Servings: 8

Ingredients:
- two cups of chicken breasts, boneless, skinless, cooked and shredded
- ten fluid ounces of enchilada sauce
- one-quarter of a teaspoon of salt
- one-quarter of a teaspoon of black pepper
- one-quarter of a cup of sour cream
- half a teaspoon of garlic powder
- half a teaspoon of cumin
- one tablespoon of cilantro, fresh, chopped
- one and a half cups of green bell pepper diced
- 15 ounces of pinto beans, canned, rinse and drain
- three-quarter of a teaspoon of chili powder
- three-quarters of a cup of onion diced
- three cups of brown rice
- ten ounces of tomatoes diced with green chilies

Directions:

In a mixing bowl combine all of the ingredients. Pour into baking pan and bake at 375° Fahrenheit for about 40 minutes. You can cool it then divide into eight portions and put them into freezer bags, label, and freeze.

17. Vegetable & Grilled Chicken Bowls

Servings: 8

Ingredients:
- four cups of cauliflower florets, roasted
- four cups of broccoli, roasted
- four cups of asparagus, roasted and chopped
- four cups of haricot beans
- four cups of roasted corn
- four cups of Brussels sprouts, roasted
- 32 ounces of grilled lime taco chicken, cubed
- 16 ounces of brown rice, cooked
- 16 ounces of quinoa, cooked

Directions:

For each bowl put in one-quarter of a cup of brown rice, one-quarter of a cup of quinoa. Top with one and a half cups of cooked veggies. To roast the veggies, you can put them onto a large baking sheet and lightly drizzle them with olive oil and salt and pepper. Cook in the oven at 375° Fahrenheit or until they are tender. Cooking time will depend on the veggie. Add half a cup of cubed chicken.

You can store the cooked meal in the fridge for up to five days.

18. Zucchini Crescent Pie

Servings: 4

Ingredients:
- three-quarter cups of canned garbanzo beans or chickpeas, drained, rinsed
- two teaspoons of parsley, fresh, chopped
- two eggs, beaten
- two cups of zucchini diced
- half a cup of onion diced
- half a teaspoon of black pepper
- half a teaspoon of garlic powder
- half a teaspoon of salt
- one-quarter cups of butter
- one-quarter teaspoon of basil, dried
- one-quarter teaspoon of oregano, dried
- one cup of Roma tomatoes, sliced
- eight ounces of crescent rolls, refrigerated
- eight ounces of mozzarella cheese, shredded

Directions:

Divide the crescent dough into triangles. Place the dough into a nine-inch pie plate with the points of the dough towards the center of pie plate. Press the bottom and sides to form a crust. Seal all the seams and perforations. Bake at 375° for eight minutes or until they are lightly browned. Sauté onion, and zucchini in butter in a large pan until tender. Stir in your seasonings. Spoon fill your crust.

In a bowl mix cheese, eggs, beans. Pour over zucchini mixes in the pie crust. Top with slices of tomato. Bake at 375° Fahrenheit for 25 minutes. Allow to stand for five minutes then cut into slices.

If you want to freeze this dish for another day, follow directions up until adding tomatoes. Do not add tomatoes or bake. Instead tightly cover the dish with foil and freeze for another day.

19. Paleo Lunch

Servings: 4

Ingredients:
- one and a half cups of zucchini, grated
- one and a half cups of ground beef, cooked
- two cups of marinara sauce
- one-quarter of a teaspoon of sea salt
- one-quarter of a teaspoon of black pepper
- one-quarter of a cup of celery diced
- half a cup of onion, diced
- half a cup of carrot, grated
- one teaspoon of basil, dried

Directions:

In a skillet add in beef, onions, and celery and cook for five minutes over medium-high heat. Add the marinara sauce, basil, salt, pepper, carrots, and zucchini. Simmer for a good ten minutes then removes from heat.

You can allow cooling and then divide meal into four portions and put into freezer bags and label and save for another day.

20. Chicken Soup with Napa Cabbage & Bok Choy

Servings: 4

Ingredients:
- five cups of chicken broth
- three teaspoons of garlic, minced
- two cups of Napa cabbage, diced
- two cups of Bok Choy, chopped
- two cups of chicken breasts, boneless, skinless, cooked and shredded
- half a cup of carrots, grated
- one tablespoon of lime juice
- one tablespoon of coconut oil
- one and a half tablespoons of ginger, fresh, peeled, minced
- two tablespoons of coconut amino's

Directions:

In a large pot over medium-high heat add in coconut oil, garlic and ginger. Sauté until they become fragrant. Add in the shredded chicken. Cook until all sides are cooked and are golden brown. Pour in the chicken stock. Add the coconut amino's. Bring to boil adding in carrots, Napa cabbage, and Bok Choy. Cook until Bok Choy is wilted. Remove from heat stir in fresh lime juice.

Allow soup to cool, divide into four portions and add to freezer bags and label.

Dinner Recipes

21. Winter Beef Stew

Servings: 2

Ingredients:
- one pound of stewing beef, cubed
- three Yukon gold potatoes, cubed
- one cup of red wine
- two celery stalks, finely sliced
- two large carrots, cut into thin coins
- one large white onion sliced finely
- butter
- one and a half tablespoons of flour
- 500ml of beef stock, low-sodium

Directions:

In a large pot, melt about one tablespoon of butter over medium heat. Add some sea salt to beef cubes and add them to the pot. Brown the beef cubes on all sides. Add more butter if needed. Remove the beef from the pot and set aside. Add in carrots, onion, and celery to pot brown these for about fifteen minutes. Add half of the wine and scrape the bottom of pot. Add back in the beef cubes to pot along with potatoes and cover with beef stock. Add in the rest of the wine. Reduce the heat to simmer for two hours.

Near the end of cooking process, mix flour with a few tablespoons of cold water in small bowl, removing lumps. Add into the pot and blend and simmer for another ten minutes.

Suggestions:

If you have any veggies laying around that need to be used, chop them up and add them to the stew as well. You do not have to add in the flour but doing this will help thicken the sauce. Then you will be able to soak a nice piece of bread into it.

This dish will take a bit more time to prepare but it is certainly well worth the effort. You can make a large batch, freeze half for another meal. You just need to double up on the recipe.

22. **Veggie Fajitas**

Servings: 2

Ingredients:
- slice half a white onion into thin strips
- half a teaspoon of garlic, minced
- one ear of corn, boiled and cut off the cob
- one red bell pepper cut into long strips
- salt and pepper to taste
- one tablespoon of butter
- taco seasoning—I use Old El Paso products
- salsa
- old cheddar cheese, grated
- one-quarter cups of rice
- half a tomato, diced
- 250ml of black beans, rinsed and drained
- two whole wheat soft tortillas

Directions:

In a pot with half a cup of water in it add the rice to it. Bring this to a boil, then turn down the heat to low and cover. Cook for 40 minutes. In a large pan melt the butter over high heat, add in onions, garlic, and brown. Reduce heat to medium and add in corn, bell pepper, black beans and some salt and pepper to taste. Mix taco seasoning with about an ounce of water in a small bowl, then add this mix to the veggies. Cook for an additional five minutes. Combine the rice, cheese, veggie mix, salsa, diced tomatoes, in a tortilla wrap.

Suggestions:

You could also fry up a half pound of ground beef to add into the veggie mix. You can use any veggies in this mix. Adding beef or chicken low-sodium stock will give it a richer flavor. If you want to really indulge, you could use the three condiments: guacamole, salsa, and sour cream. With leftover tortillas, make tortilla chips if you like.

23. Simple Pita Pizza

Servings: 1

Ingredients:
- one piece of pita bread or naan bread
- spaghetti sauce
- basil, freshly chopped
- five cherry tomatoes, sliced in half
- old cheddar or mozzarella, shredded

Directions:

Preheat the oven to 375° Fahrenheit. Add the ingredients to the bread starting with a coating of spaghetti sauce then tomatoes, cheese then sprinkle with basil. Bake for ten minutes or until the cheese begins to bubble.

Suggestions:

Using pita or naan bread are great for making a quick pizza. Add whatever you would like for toppings such as some leftovers from your dinner from the night before.

24. Szechuan Chicken Stir Fry

Servings: 1

Ingredients:
- one-third cup of rice
- one chicken breast, skinless, boneless, finely chopped
- one teaspoon of ginger, finely grated
- a handful of mushrooms, sliced
- half of a red bell pepper cut into chunks
- one green onion, chopped
- a few pieces of broccoli cut into small pieces
- half of a white onion, cut into chunks
- one carrot cut into coins
- Szechuan Stir Fry Sauce
- a handful of unsalted peanuts
- pepper to taste
- one tablespoon of olive oil
- one teaspoon of garlic, minced

Directions:

In a pot with two-thirds of a cup of cold water with rice, bring to a boil. Then cover and set to simmer for 35 minutes. Over medium-high heat in a large pan, heat up olive oil. Add in minced garlic and ginger mix for a few minutes. Add in the pieces of chicken and cook on all sides until nice and brown. Add in the onion cooking for an additional five minutes. Once the onion is browned, add in other veggies and cook for an additional ten minutes. Add in pepper to taste. Add in Szechuan sauce and mix well. Serve over a bed of rice.

Options:

This is a great meal if you have a bunch of random veggies in your fridge that you want to use up. You might even add in other things to this dish such as pork, beef or shrimp. Among other great veggies that will work well are celery, snow peas, jalapenos, and bamboo shoots.

25. Mango & Grainy Mustard Salmon

Servings: 1

Ingredients:
- one salmon fillet
- sea salt to taste
- one ripe mango, cubed
- few slices of red onion
- one tablespoon of grainy mustard
- one-third of a cup of brown rice
- pepper to taste

Directions:

Add in a pot two-thirds cup of cold water and rice, bring to boil. Lower heat and cover cooking on simmer for 40 minutes. Spread the grainy mustard on one side of the salmon fillet. Make a foil parcel with salmon, sea salt, pepper, red onion, and mango cubes bake at 350° Fahrenheit for 15 minutes. Add some salt and pepper to rice. Place the salmon fillet on a bed of rice.

Suggestions:

If the mango is not very sweet you could sprinkle some brown sugar onto it. If you have a fresh lemon, squeeze some of it onto the salmon in the parcel. You can also add some small matchstick carrots into a parcel. In case there are leftover mango, use these to make a salsa.

26. South American Whole Wheat Burrito

Servings: 1

Ingredients:
- one tablespoon of apple cider vinegar
- one tablespoon of white onion, finely chopped
- two tortilla shells
- one can of refried beans
- hot sauce to taste
- juice of two limes
- one-third of a head of cabbage, thinly chopped
- salt and pepper to taste

Directions:

You can make a simple fat-free coleslaw by mixing cabbage, lime juice, carrot, onion, and vinegar in a large bowl. In a large pan, heat the refried beans over medium heat. Once the beans are hot, add a layer of beans on one side of the tortilla shell and add a handful of coleslaw and some hot sauce and roll up the burrito.

Suggestions:

Once you have rolled up the burritos, you can then put them onto a baking sheet and bake at 400° Fahrenheit for a few minutes to crisp the shells. Add in some slices of old cheddar. If you have any leftover chicken or beef, you could also add these to get some protein.

27. Turkey with Green Bean Casserole

Servings: 8

Ingredients:
- one cup of turkey
- ten cups of green beans
- one and a half cups of parsnips
- one and a half cups of chicken broth
- salt and pepper to taste
- two and a quarter of a cups of cremini mushrooms, sliced
- eight tablespoons of shallots, diced
- one cup of white onion, sliced
- five teaspoons of garlic, minced
- two tablespoons of ghee

Directions:

Over medium heat in a large saucepan, put in the parsnips. Cover with water and boil. Simmer for 20 minutes. In another saucepan, add in the green beans and bring to boil. Simmer for 20 minutes. Drain the parsnips and green beans, set aside.

In a large skillet, heat ghee adding in the garlic, onions, shallots, mushrooms, pepper and salt. Cook until the mushrooms are brown. Place half of the mushrooms and cooked parsnips into the food processor and blend until smooth. Add turkey to green beans mix in skillet. Pour mixed greens into a baking pan. Pour blended sauce over the top. Bake at 375° Fahrenheit for 30 minutes or until the puree is bubbling.

Snack Recipes

31. Oat Parfait

Servings: 1

Ingredients:
- one cup of quick oats
- three tablespoons of walnuts
- two third of a cup of mango
- one third of a cup of unsweetened almond milk
- half a cup of Greek yogurt, plain

Directions:

Add into mason jar milk and oats. Mix well. Top this with yogurt, mango, and nuts. Place on the lid. Refrigerate for overnight. You can serve this snack cold or warm.

This snack can be prepared ahead and kept in the fridge for up to five days. ☐

32. Lemon Blueberry Chia Pudding

Servings: 1

Ingredients:
- three tablespoons of Chia seeds
- two teaspoons of honey
- one quarter of a cup of Greek yogurt
- one teaspoon of vanilla extract
- half a cup of blueberries, frozen or fresh
- half a cup of almond milk
- half a lemon, juice and zest

Directions:

Put the Chia seeds, milk, yogurt, lemon juice and zest, honey and vanilla extract in a mason jar with lid. Keep this in the fridge overnight. When ready to eat, you just need to stir. Top with blueberries if you like.

33. Chocolate Chia Pudding

Servings: 1

Ingredients:
- four tablespoons of Chia seeds
- three quarter of a cup of almond milk
- two teaspoons of honey
- one teaspoon of vanilla extract
- one tablespoon of cocoa powder

Directions:

Put Chia seeds in milk, honey, vanilla extract, and cocoa powder mix in mason jar and place on the lid. Leave overnight in the fridge, stir and enjoy. You can make this up to five days ahead.□

34. Oatmeal White Chocolate Cookies

Servings: 18

Ingredients:
- three cups of all-purpose flour
- two eggs
- two teaspoons of vanilla extract
- two cups of white chocolate chips
- one teaspoon of salt
- one teaspoon of baking powder
- one cup of brown sugar
- one and a half cups of rolled oats
- one cup of pecans
- one cup of margarine
- one teaspoon of baking soda

Directions:

Mix margarine and sugar until nice and creamy. Whisk the eggs and vanilla. Add in the flour, baking soda, salt, and baking powder; mix them well. Stir in the oats and chocolate chips. Roll into golf ball size and put onto ungreased cookie sheets. Bake at 350° Fahrenheit for about twelve minutes.

Allow the cookies to cool and then you can put some in freezer bags to keep for another day. □

35. Chocolate Sundae Cookies

Servings: 18

Ingredients:
- one and a half cups of all-purpose flour
- half a cup of shortening
- one teaspoon of vanilla
- one egg
- two thirds of a cup of brown sugar
- two tablespoons of milk
- two ounces of unsweetened chocolate
- ten regular marshmallows, cut in half
- one quarter of a cup of maraschino cherry juice
- one quarter of a cup of maraschino cherries, drained, chopped
- half a teaspoon of salt
- half a teaspoon of baking soda
- half a cup of walnuts, chopped
- 35 maraschino cherries

For the glaze:
- six ounces of semi-sweet chocolate
- four tablespoons of shortening
- one quarter of a teaspoon of vanilla extract
- four teaspoons of corn syrup

Directions:

In a large bowl, whisk egg, half cup of shortening, brown sugar, and one teaspoon vanilla. Melt chocolate and pour into bowl with whisked egg mix. Add flour, baking soda, milk, salt, one quarter cup of chopped cherries, walnuts, and cherry juice. Mix well. Scoop teaspoonful onto greased cookie sheets. Bake at 350° Fahrenheit for twelve minutes. Melt chocolate chips. Add in four tablespoons of shortening and corn syrup. Mix. Remove from heat. Stir in vanilla. Remove cookies from oven, press half a marshmallow into the center.

Allow to cool for ten minutes. Spoon glaze over cookies and top with cherry. When totally cool, freeze some in freezer bags for another day.

36. Peanut Butter Swirl & Banana Muffins

Servings: 12

Ingredients:
- three bananas, ripe, mashed
- one and one quarter of a teaspoon of baking powder
- one third of a cup of smooth peanut butter
- half a teaspoon of cinnamon
- one cup of protein powder, vanilla
- one cup of quick oats
- one teaspoon of pure vanilla extract
- half a cup of almond milk
- half a cup of unsweetened applesauce
- half a teaspoon of baking soda

Swirl:
- three tablespoons of peanut butter

Directions:

Preheat the oven to 375° and grease a non-stick 12-muffin tin with cooking spray. Set aside. In a large mixing bowl whisk peanut butter, milk, mashed bananas, applesauce, and vanilla extract. Add in the oats, protein powder, baking soda, baking powder, and cinnamon. Fill tin with two thirds mix. Bake for 20 minutes. Remove from tins. Allow to cool. Can keep in fridge for up to five days.

37. **Coconut Custard**

Servings: 8

Ingredients:
- 5 egg yolks
- 13 ounces of canned coconut milk
- one quarter cup of coconut flour
- one and a half cups of coconut cream
- one cup of applesauce
- one cup of coconut flakes, toasted
- one tablespoon of maple syrup
- half a teaspoon of cardamom, ground
- half a teaspoon of sea salt
- one quarter of a cup of arrowroot powder

Topping:
- half a cup of blueberries
- half a cup of blackberries

Directions:

In a mixing bowl whisk egg yolks, coconut cream, coconut milk, applesauce, and maple syrup. In another bowl add arrowroot powder, sea salt, coconut flour and cardamom. Whisk the dry ingredients and add them into wet ingredients and mix well. Pour the mix into a pan of 9×13 (baking dish) and bake at 350° Fahrenheit for 50 minutes or until it has set. Sprinkle the top of custard with toasted coconut flakes and top with berries.

Once the custard has cooled, you can cut it into 8 pieces and wrap in individual plastic cups cover with plastic wrap and freeze for another day.

38. Yummy Nutty Banana & Oatmeal Bars

Servings: 9

Ingredients:
- six dates, pitted, chopped
- one teaspoon of baking powder
- half a cup of almond milk
- half a teaspoon of baking soda
- half a teaspoon of cinnamon
- one quarter of a cup of flax seed, ground
- one quarter of a teaspoon of salt
- two cups of old fashioned rolled oats
- one cup of applesauce, unsweetened
- one cup of bananas, ripe, mashed
- optional – one quarter of a cup of chocolate chips
- half a cup of walnuts, chopped

Directions:

Preheat the oven to 375° Fahrenheit. Line the baking dish with parchment paper. Spray it with non-stick cooking spray. In a bowl mix applesauce, milk and bananas. Add in the rest of the ingredients, except the walnuts. Pour the mix into a baking dish, level the mix using a spatula.   Top with chocolate chips, if you wish and then bake for 40 minutes or until you can stick a knife in it and it comes out clean.

Remove from the oven and allow to cool. Cut into eight bars, serve warm or cold with yogurt or peanut butter. Place the bars into an airtight container and freeze up to three months.☐

39. Tasty Pumpkin Roll

Servings: 8

Ingredients:
- three eggs
- two thirds of a cup of pumpkin, canned
- one teaspoon of baking soda
- three quarter of a cup of all-purpose flour
- one cup of white sugar
- half a cup of walnuts (optional)

For Filling:
- eight ounces of cream cheese
- two tablespoons of butter, softened
- one cup of powdered sugar
- three quarters of a teaspoon of vanilla extract

Directions:

Preheat the oven to 375° Fahrenheit. Spray a 10x15 inch jelly-roll pan with non-stick cooking spray. Line with parchment paper. In a large bowl, mix eggs for five minutes on high with blender. Add in the sugar and pumpkin. Add in the flour, baking soda, and cinnamon. Spread the batter inside of pan with a spatula. Sprinkle in the walnuts on top. Bake for 15 minutes. Dust a linen towel with powdered sugar. Mix filling ingredients.

When the cake is baked, turn in over onto the dusted linen towel. Peel off parchment paper. Starting with the short end of cake, roll up the cake in the towel. Carefully unroll the cake. Spread the filling over, within about an inch from edges. Roll it up again. Cover and refrigerate until serving.

To freeze this yummy snack, you can roll it in wax paper and then in foil. Seal all the edges. Put inside a large freezer bag.☐

40. Applesauce Waffles

Servings: 14

Ingredients:
- two cups of oat flour (finely ground quick oats)
- two cups of almond meal (finely ground nuts)
- one and a half cups of applesauce, unsweetened
- one large egg
- one and a quarter cups of almond milk
- one teaspoon of vanilla extract
- one quarter of a cup of flax seed, ground
- half a teaspoon of salt
- one teaspoon of baking soda
- half a cup of raw honey

Directions:

In a mixing bowl, beat the eggs lightly. Add in honey, baking soda, applesauce, flax seed, and vanilla. Whisk together until well blended. Add in the oat flour and the almond meal. Mix well. Now preheat the waffle maker. With cooking spray, grease the top and bottom of the griddle. Cook the waffles.

You can put them into an air-circulating container and store them for up to six months.

Chapter 7: Clean Eating Meal Prep Recipes

1. **Sweet Potato Brownies**

Servings: 12

Ingredients:
- two large sweet potatoes
- half a cup of quinoa flour
- two eggs
- one and a half teaspoons of baking powder
- half a cup of cocoa powder
- one zucchini, skinned, cubed
- three egg whites
- one third of a cup of organic honey

Directions:

Preheat the oven to 415° Fahrenheit. Bake the sweet potatoes for about one hour or until they are soft. Allow them to cool at room temperature.

Preheat oven to 350° Fahrenheit. In a large bowl, add in the sweet potatoes with all of the other ingredients and mash. Evenly divide this mix into muffin pan and bake for 30 minutes, or until toothpick when inserted into brownies comes out clean. ☐

2. Grilled Chicken Breast & Stuffed Sweet Potatoes

Serving Size: 1 potato and one chicken breast per person

Ingredients:
- two pounds of chicken breast, skinless, boneless
- two third of whole bell peppers, red and green
- one cup of corn
- one cup of black beans
- three sweet potatoes
- three green onions, chopped
- one zucchini, chopped into small pieces
- five tablespoons of mozzarella cheese, shredded
- seasonings: paprika, cayenne, sea salt and pepper
- one cup of broccoli
- one teaspoon of garlic, minced

Directions:

Preheat the oven to 405° Fahrenheit. Wrap the sweet potatoes up in aluminum foil and bake for about 50 minutes. Season the chicken with Mrs. Dash Chipotle, paprika, sea salt, pepper, and cayenne and cook in a non-stick skillet and set aside. Chop up the veggies into small pieces. Saute corn and garlic in a non-stick pan using a coconut oil spray. Once the corn is seared, toss in the beans and veggies. Slice the sweet potatoes in half and carve out a pocket in the middle of them. Set aside the portions that you carved out to use later. Fill the inside of the sweet potatoes with veggie mixture, then top them with one tablespoon of mozzarella. Bake for eight minutes at 405° Fahrenheit. Serve with chicken breasts.☐

3. Breakfast Omelet Roll-Ups

Servings: 1

Ingredients:
- one whole egg
- four egg whites
- one handful of spinach, chopped
- three ounces of lean ground turkey
- one third of a cup of bell pepper, diced
- one ounce of goat cheese

Directions:

In a skillet, you can cook the lean ground turkey and drain. In another skillet, cook the egg along with egg whites. Add in the goat cheese, spinach, bell peppers and the ground turkey. Roll up mixture once cooled into plastic wrap and refrigerate until you are ready to heat it up and eat it. □

4. Balsamic Chicken

Servings: 12

Ingredients:
- three pounds of chicken breast, skinless, boneless
- four tablespoons of balsamic vinegar
- one tablespoon of red chili sauce
- one teaspoon of ginger, grated
- one tablespoon of organic honey

Directions:

Preheat the oven to 405° Fahrenheit. In a small bowl mix the honey, chili sauce and balsamic dressing along with ginger. Place the chicken in a Ziploc bag, adding in the mix. Shake to coat chicken and marinate for 20 minutes. Place chicken pieces on baking sheet and bake for 15 minutes. ☐

5. Lean Turkey Lasagna Meal Prep

Servings: 3

Ingredients:
- one pound of lean ground turkey
- one and a half cups of marinara sauce
- three quarters of a cup of mozzarella cheese, shredded
- one egg white
- one cup of cottage cheese
- season with garlic powder
- one zucchini, diced

Directions:

Preheat the oven to 350° Fahrenheit. Season the ground turkey and cook in a skillet, add in marinara sauce and stir. Slice zucchini into small pieces. Mix in a bowl the cottage cheese and the egg white. In a baking tray, add one layer of zucchini, meat sauce, and cottage cheese and top with mozzarella. Bake for 30 minutes, then allow to cool and divide into three containers for three prep meals.

Conclusion

I hope that you gain much pleasure and enjoyment out of trying my recipes collection. My main goal was to provide tips and suggestions that will help you in developing your meal prep skills. Once you get into the swing of things, you will find that life will feel so much less stressful when you are not worrying about what you have to throw together for dinner when you get home from a long day at work. Instead, you can feel good in knowing that you have done some meal preps, and you have stored up a nice selection of foods to choose from to provide yourself and your family members with tasty, nutritious home-cooked meals.

And let us not forget you will be saving time and money when you are organized in your meal preps. I wish you the best success in developing your own meals plans. I hope that you will use the tips and suggestions that I have offered in this book to help guide you during your journey to better meal planning.

I would like to thank you once again for downloading this book, your support of my work means a great deal to me. I would love to read a review by you of this book on Amazon.

Happy Meal Prepping!

Other Related Books

	Meal Prep: The Ultimate Guide for Beginners - Everything You Need to Know About Prepping Delicious and Healthy Meals! ASIN: B01FR6TKD4
	Operation Dinner: How to Plan, Shop & Prep for Easy Family Meals ASIN: B00CKCL52I
	Binge Eating: A Self-Help Guide to Recovery from Eating Disorder ASIN: B01F11ZRK0 ISBN-13: 978-1532955730
	Binge Eating Disorder: Proven Strategies & Treatments to Stop Over Eating ASIN: B011QYCCNG ISBN-13: 978-1519547088

Made in the USA
Middletown, DE
26 September 2023

39454542R00046